# The Hamster Problem

Written by Suzy Senior

Illustrated by Noopur Thakur

**Collins**

"Freena, can you help?" yells Gran.
"We have a slight problem.
Star is missing."

Star is my sleek, brown hamster.
She is an expert at getting free.

"Is she asleep in the bed in the hamster tank?" I ask.

Gran snorts, "No. Star left a trail."

She points to the trail of fluff and mess
on the carpet.

We start looking. I creep under the green stool.

No Star here!

Gran sweeps a soft broom under the bench.

Do not frighten her.

No Star there!

Then we clear some painting things off the stairs. Still no Star!

Just then, my dog Storm starts fussing. He is sniffing Gran's trainer.

Gran frowns. "Freena, get Storm. His drool will spoil my trainers," she groans.

I speed across and grab Storm.

But there is a sleek, brown lump sleeping in Gran's trainer!

The lump uncurls. It is my lost hamster, Star!

There you are, Star!

I scoop Star out and lift her back into the tank.

"Thank you, Storm. Clever dog!" exclaims Gran.

# What did Star do?

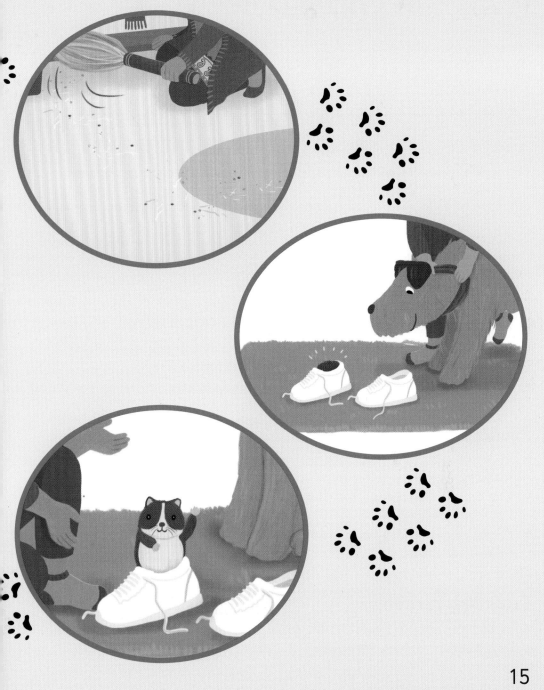

# After reading

**Letters and Sounds:** Phase 4

**Word count:** 170

Focus on adjacent consonants with long vowel phonemes, e.g. *clear.*

**Common exception words:** of, to, the, no, I, into, are, my, she, we, you, have, do, some, there, here, ask, out

**Curriculum links:** Science: Animals, including humans

**National Curriculum learning objectives:** Reading/word reading: apply phonic knowledge and skills as the route to decode words; read accurately by blending sounds in unfamiliar words containing GPCs that have been taught; read common exception words, noting unusual correspondences between spelling and sound and where these occur in the word; read other words of more than one syllable that contain taught GPCs; Reading/comprehension: understand both the books they can already read accurately and fluently and those they listen to by making inferences on the basis of what is being said and done

## Developing fluency

- Read the book together, encouraging your child to reread sentences if they have difficulty with exception words, such as **there** and **here**.
- You could ask your child to read the story as Freena, the narrator, and you just read Gran's spoken words.

## Phonic practice

- Encourage your child to practise reading words that contain adjacent consonants with long vowels.
- Turn to page 10 and point to **trainers**. Ask your child to sound out and blend the word. (/t/ /r/ /ai/ /n/ /er/ /s/)
- Challenge your child to read these words with more than one syllable, breaking them down if necessary:

  ex-pert      as-leep      fright-en      paint-ing      sleep-ing

## Extending vocabulary

- Reread the following pages and discuss the meaning of these words:

  page 2 **yells**      page 10 **groans**      page 13 **exclaims**

- Discuss other words you can use instead of "said". (e.g. *moaned, whispered, cried, giggled, called, shouted*)